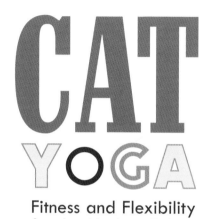

CAT YOGA

Fitness and Flexibility for the Modern Feline

CAT
YOGA

Fitness and Flexibility
for the Modern Feline

Rick Tillotson

Photography by David Carroll

Clarkson Potter/Publishers
New York

Published in the United States by Clarkson Potter/Publishers, an imprint of
the Crown Publishing Group, a division of Random House, Inc., New York.
www.crownpublishing.com
www.clarksonpotter.com
Clarkson N. Potter is a trademark and Potter and colophon are registered
trademarks of Random House, Inc.

Library of Congress Cataloging-in-Publication Data
Tillotson, Rick.
Cat yoga: fitness and flexibility for the modern feline / Rick Tillotson—1st ed.
1. Cats—Humor. 2. Yoga—Humor. I. Title.
PN6231.C23T55 2007
818'.602—dc22   2007013133

ISBN 978-0-307-35254-5

Printed in Singapore
Design by Danielle Deschenes
Photography by David Carroll

10 9 8 7 6 5 4 3 2 1
First Edition

For Mom

Introduction

Many years ago I was a teacher of yoga in a humble community about a hundred miles east of Jaipur in Northern India. At that time it was my great privilege to have met Purusha (as I called him), one of many cats who lived on the outskirts of our small town. Despite the number of felines surrounding our community, I always seemed to take notice of Purusha. Perhaps this was because he was smaller, skinnier, and appeared less coordinated or "sure-footed" than other cats. Or maybe it was because he frequently seemed on the losing end of a conflict over food, or a fight with another cat. But more than that, I think he interested me because of how he would look at me when I saw him . . . almost as if he had something he wanted to ask me. Frequently I would see him walking by the yoga studio and watching from afar, possibly wondering what was happening inside.

One evening, after all my students had left and I was about to close for the day, I saw Purusha sitting quietly outside the doorway, looking at me in his inquisitive way. After a few moments of our regarding each other, he tilted his head slightly and waved his tail behind him. Somehow I understood this to be a form of request, and I opened my hands as an invitation for him to enter. He seemed to understand my gesture, as he silently rose, walked through the doorway, and sat directly in front of me. He did not seem remotely afraid of me, so I lowered myself to sit in front of him, noticing at once his uneven fur, broken whiskers, and small scars—undoubtedly from his conflicts with other cats.

What happened next I had never seen a cat do before. Purusha slowly stood on his hind legs and raised both paws in the air. He sat like this for only a few seconds before he lost his balance and fell forward. Intrigued, I lifted my own arms in the air and raised up on my knees in front of him to mimic his original position. He watched me closely as I did this, and again raised his arms. This time, however, he appeared steady and maintained the posture almost twice as long. After this unusual exchange, Purusha performed another unimaginable feat. He got up from his seated position, stood before me on his four legs, and then proceeded to raise one rear leg backward while raising his opposite front leg forward. I was astounded! This posture was obviously a difficult one for him, as he quickly lost balance and went back to four paws on the ground, but again he watched me as I mimicked the pose, and then performed it himself with greater ease and balance. I began to understand that Purusha wanted to learn yoga!

From then on, Purusha would meet me every evening to practice the yoga postures that he spied my students performing through the studio windows during the day. It was a mystery to me why a cat would want to learn yoga, but as the weeks passed, I watched Purusha transform. When I saw him around the village, his head and tail were held high. He had gained weight and his coat appeared glowing and healthy. His peace and gracefulness now exceeded that of the natural gifts most felines have as their birthright, and I noticed that his relationships with his peers were harmonious and without conflict. Indeed, I saw that other cats greatly respected and looked up to him, perhaps curious of his secret. For that reason I was not surprised to eventually find other cats with Purusha at the door of my studio—wanting to learn cat yoga.

Since then cat yoga has continued to grow in popularity as cats learn the special benefits that yoga affords them in their daily lives, including increased flexibility, balance, and stress relief. Purusha and I continue to practice yoga together, and we are honored to share the benefits we have discovered with you.

VIRABHADRASANA

This posture, also known as *Warrior Pose*, strengthens the legs and back. Cats are known for being able to spring over six times their own length, but cat yogis who practice this posture can reportedly jump even farther.

PARIGHASANA

A primary benefit of *Crossbar Pose* is a stretch of the muscles surrounding the rib cage. These muscles can become especially tense during territory negotiations outside the house, or anywhere that growling is required.

BAKASANA

The *Crane Pose* strengthens the muscles of the legs and hips. The cat's most powerful muscles are in the hindquarters, allowing felines to spring long distances to attack their dinner or favorite cat toy.

ANANTASANA

The *Side-Lying Leg Raise* stretches the muscles of the pelvis and can lessen discomfort prior to (and following) the delivery of kittens. Always check with your veterinarian before beginning any exercise program while carrying a litter.

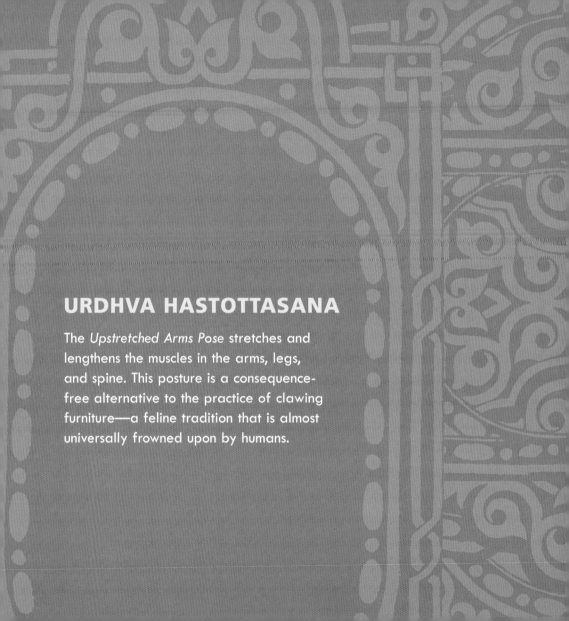

URDHVA HASTOTTASANA

The *Upstretched Arms Pose* stretches and lengthens the muscles in the arms, legs, and spine. This posture is a consequence-free alternative to the practice of clawing furniture—a feline tradition that is almost universally frowned upon by humans.

URDHVA PADASANA

Neutered cats can often gain weight since they no longer expend the energy necessary to search for a mate. The *Raised Foot Pose* is a good posture for cats who are just beginning a yoga exercise program to lose unwanted pounds.

ARDHA USHTRASANA

Also known as *Half-Camel Pose*, this posture
stretches the stomach and intestines. In
longer haired cats, this pose assists in the
passing of hairballs.

BAKA DHYANASANA

The *Patient Crane Posture* requires the kind of balance and poise for which most felines are known. As a cat's tail is a primary tool in its balance, cats with a short tail (or no tail, such as the Bobtail pictured here) can make up for their handicap by studying balance poses such as this one.

BILIKASANA

This is a slight variation on the human yoga pose known as *Cat Posture*. While cat yogis appreciate their recognition in the name of this posture, simply posing as a cat (as the human posture entails) is slightly boring for them—so they prefer the variation.

HALASANA

The *Plow Pose* stimulates the thyroid glands (located in the neck) by compressing the head against the chest. The thyroid glands regulate metabolism and appetite, and an imbalance can result in either an excessively skinny or a "plus-size" cat.

MERUDANDASANA

Also known as *Balancing Bear Pose*, this posture stimulates the internal organs, in particular the liver. The feline liver is different from the human, or even the canine, liver in that it needs animal protein in order to function properly—there are no vegetarian cats.

ADVASANA

Reversed Corpse Pose is another posture that can help rehabilitate an injured back. Human practitioners are advised to press their navel into the floor. Instead of navels, felines have a small scar along the rib cage from where they were connected to their mother.

TIRYAKA TADASANA

The *Swaying Palm Tree Pose* provides a good stretch of the lateral muscles of the torso while improving balance. Cat yogis who regularly enjoy chasing their tails often use this pose as a warm-up.

MUKTA HASTA MERUDANDASANA

This posture, often referred to as the *Rocking Horse Pose*, provides a strong contraction of the abdominal muscles. Regular practice of this pose is helpful for cats trying to develop a "six-pack."

ASVATTASANA

The *Holy Fig Tree Posture* is said to improve energy and circulation. While the average cat would prefer to climb a tree rather than pose like one, cat yogis enjoy doing both.

PARIVRTTA SASAMGASANA

The *Reverse Hare Posture* requires a twisting of the torso, which massages and stimulates the internal organs.

MARICYASANA

The *Standing Spinal Twist* is another pose that focuses on the joints and muscles of the spine. Unlike in humans, the feline's flexible spine and supple muscles allow it to turn up to 180 degrees in emergency situations (such as turning in midair to land on its feet).

UTTIHITA HASTA PADANGUSTHASANA

A member of the Scottish Fold breed (known for their ears, which appear to be folded downward) demonstrates this pose, which is also known as *Extended Hand-to-Toe Posture*. Appropriate tail positioning is critical in maintaining balance in such poses.

SARPASANA

This posture, also known as *Snake Pose*, creates increased pressure in the chest cavity and helps to strengthen the muscles of the heart. When cats encounter real snakes, strong muscles are required to keep the cat's heart from beating out of its chest.

SETU BANDHASANA

A relatively easy posture for humans, the *Bridge Pose* is more difficult for cats, as it requires a complete rotation of the feline hip. Only the most advanced cat yogis are able to achieve this posture.

GATYATMAK MERU VAKRASANA

Cats who carry a lot of excess weight often suffer from back pain. Poses such as the *Dynamic Spinal Twist* help stretch and strengthen the muscles of the back, while simultaneously burning a few calories.

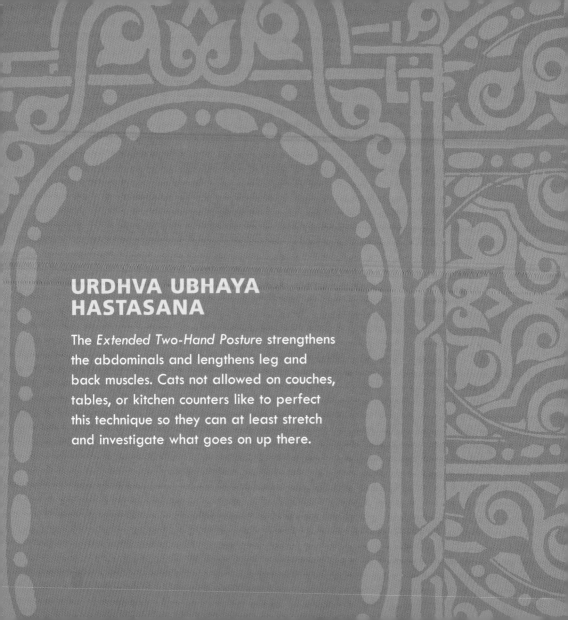

URDHVA UBHAYA HASTASANA

The *Extended Two-Hand Posture* strengthens the abdominals and lengthens leg and back muscles. Cats not allowed on couches, tables, or kitchen counters like to perfect this technique so they can at least stretch and investigate what goes on up there.

TRIKONASANA

The sideways stretch provided by *Triangle Pose* activates the muscles of the trunk and is said to stimulate the central nervous system and alleviate depression. If your cat appears to be losing interest in chasing birds or isn't pacing around the food bowl, this pose is recommended.

ARDHA CHANDRASANA

Felines are nocturnal animals, and therefore are most active at night. The *Half-Moon Pose* is a posture that holds a special place in the heart of the nighttime hunter.

UPAVISTHA KONASANA

Also known as the *Wide-Angle Seated Forward Bend*, this pose helps open the muscles surrounding the hips and pelvis. Practiced regularly (up to two weeks before delivering a litter), this pose can facilitate a relatively pain-free kitten birth.

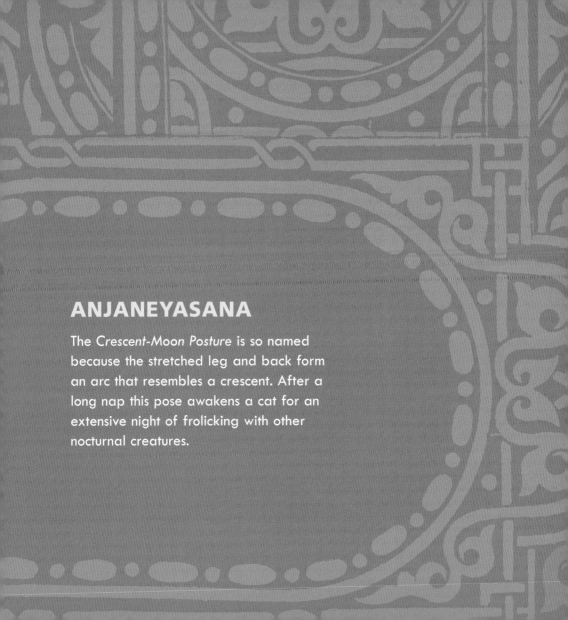

ANJANEYASANA

The *Crescent-Moon Posture* is so named because the stretched leg and back form an arc that resembles a crescent. After a long nap this pose awakens a cat for an extensive night of frolicking with other nocturnal creatures.

ADHO MUHKA DWIKONASANA

The *Downward Double-Angle Pose* provides a nice stretch of the arms, shoulders, and upper back. This posture is good for adolescent cats who are learning to jump down from high places, as these muscles act as their primary shock absorbers.

URDHVA HASTA SARVANGASANA

Upward Forward-Bend Pose is one of many poses that improve circulation to the head and upper body. Postures such as this stimulate increased blood flow to the brain and can induce a state of well-being that often results in spontaneous purring.

PRANAMASANA

This posture, also known as *Prayer Pose*, is used to establish concentration and a sense of calm prior to beginning a yoga routine. Among the things that cats pray for are warm laps, a variety of cat toys, and delicious saucers of milk.

PRARAMBHIK STHITI

One of the benefits of *Base Posture* is that it generally stimulates the various endocrine glands of the cat. Also known as the hormonal system, these glands regulate two of the cat's favorite activities—eating and sleeping.

PARIVRTTA UTTHITA HASTASANA

Reverse Raised-Arms Pose stretches the muscles of the torso while expanding the chest cavity. Cats who spend a lot of time running from neighborhood canines can benefit from the increased lung capacity that this posture develops.

DWIKONASANA

The *Double-Angle Posture* stretches almost
every muscle in the body. The inverted
arms provide the added benefit of
increasing blood flow to the brain, which
can help improve memory and can benefit
older cats that seem to have forgotten the
location of the litter box.

ARDHA HASTASANA

The *Half Handstand* is a difficult pose for humans to achieve. Cats, however, have less weight in their legs and don't require as much counterbalance. This posture is a favorite for felines who wish to show their superiority over their human counterparts.

NATARAJASANA

This challenging balance posture, known as *Lord Shiva's Pose*, is named after the center of the universe in Hindu mythology. Because cats often believe they hold this distinction, they are very fond of this pose.

BHUJANGASANA

A cat's famous reflexes depend on unimpeded transmission of signals from the brain to the rest of the body through the nerves in the spinal cord. Cats who practice the *Cobra Pose* on a regular basis will develop a healthier spine and live up to the cobra name with their increased speed and reflexes.

PADAHASTASANA

The *Front-to-Rear Paws Posture* lengthens and stretches the spine—a good pose for cats who wish to avoid fights to practice. In conflicts with other cats, a highly arched back can intimidate an opponent into retreat.

SAMAKONASANA

Also known as the *Right-Angle Pose*, this posture strengthens and tones the muscles of the upper back. Cats who frequently arch their backs to intimidate their opponents into retreat often develop spinal curvature or poor posture that can be corrected through regular practice of this pose.

NAUKASANA

This posture is referred to as *Boat Pose* because of its resemblance to a boat with oars. As most cats are not fond of water, this is as close to a boat as most cat yogis want to be.

VRKSASANA

The *Tree Pose* stretches and lengthens the rib cage. Cats are known for their slim rib cages, which allow them to squeeze through narrow openings. Often the span of a cat's whiskers matches the width of its body, allowing it to test where it is able to fit without getting stuck.

SANTOLANASANA

Cats are known for their flexible and agile spines. However, a miscalculated leap or a sparring session with a fellow feline can sometimes result in a slipped disk. The *Balancing Posture* relieves pressure on the spinal nerves and can help realign the spine.

URDHVA MUKA VRKSASANA

This posture, also known as *Upward-Facing Tree Pose*, has as its primary focus a strengthening of the cat's wrists. The wrists of a cat have a delicate structure that allow them to expertly grasp and manipulate cat toys or captured prey.

SHAVASANA

This posture, also known as *Corpse Pose*, should be performed at the beginning and end of each routine to completely relax every muscle. Although cats are experts at relaxing, this is not their normal position for doing so, and therefore takes a little getting used to.

SHASHANKASANA

The *Pose of the Moon* is reported to promote feelings of peace and tranquillity. Cats who regularly practice this posture are said to sleep more soundly and have a lower incidence of territory confrontations with their neighbors.

VYAGHRASANA

Even cats who don't practice traditional cat yoga can be found to practice this posture, known as *Tiger Pose*. It is so named because it is often part of the stretching routine of any member of the feline species upon waking from a long nap.

JANU SIRSASANA

The righting reflex—which allows a cat to completely flip itself in midair—requires a very flexible spine. This posture, also known as *Head-to-Knee Pose*, gives a good stretch to the spine and dorsal (back) muscles.

SARVANGASANA

An increase in blood flow to the head is a primary benefit of the *Shoulder-Stand Pose*. This posture can also be helpful in promoting the regeneration of lost whiskers— a common complaint of older cats.

AKARNA DHANURASANA

Also called the *Bow and Arrow Pose*,
this posture stretches and stimulates the
shoulder muscles. Unlike in humans, a cat's
shoulder blades are not connected to
the rest of the skeleton, making healthy
shoulder muscles critical to a cat's structure
and movement.

UTKATASANA

Cats suffering from a loose or flabby mid-section can benefit from the *Squatting Pose*. Included in a routine of other postures targeting the abdominal muscles, this pose can help to streamline a bulky torso.

VASISTHASANA

This posture is literally translated as "most excellent, best, riches," but is better known as *Side Plank Pose*. Cats with aggressive personalities or behavioral problems may benefit from this pose, as it is reported to promote inner harmony.

ARDHA SHALABHASANA

Cats with weak backs or lower-back pain can benefit from this pose, also known as the *Half-Locust Posture*. Strong back muscles are required for turning in midair while falling from tree branches, and for absorbing impact when landing.

JATHARA PARIVARTANASANA

Larger cats wishing a gradual transition from a low-activity lifestyle will appreciate the *Belly-Turning Pose*, which requires simply raising the paw and tail while otherwise remaining fully reclined.

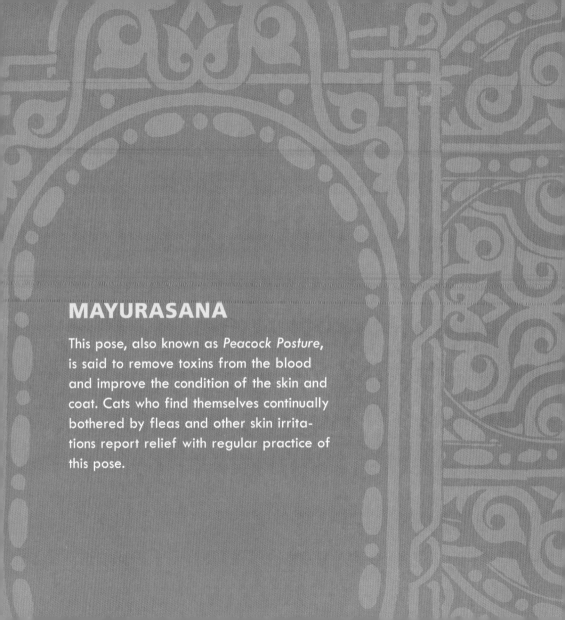

MAYURASANA

This pose, also known as *Peacock Posture*, is said to remove toxins from the blood and improve the condition of the skin and coat. Cats who find themselves continually bothered by fleas and other skin irritations report relief with regular practice of this pose.

TADAGI MUDRA

Also known as the *Barreled-Abdomen Pose*, this posture has a primary benefit of alleviating tension in the diaphragm, which can become stressed in female cats who wail for hours during mating season.

UTTHANPADASANA

Also known as *Raised Legs Pose*, this posture strengthens the abdominals and legs while stimulating digestion. It is especially helpful in eliminating the unwanted calories that come from too many cat treats.

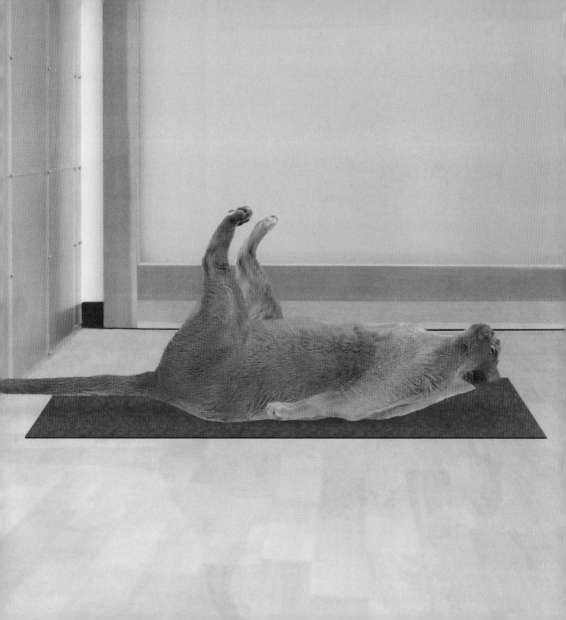

BALA TADASANA

Mountain Pose (or *Hill Pose,* in the case of kittens) is the starting point for any standing posture and is a necessary pose for any aspiring kitten yogi to master.

BALA PADAHASTASANA

The kitten version of *Front-to-Rear Paws Posture* has benefits similar to those of the adult pose. This posture develops all the muscles necessary for the feline-patented pounce attack.

BALA VIRABHADRASANA

Also known as *Young Warrior Pose*, this posture can build self-esteem in a young cat finding itself in a strange new world. It may be difficult to imagine a kitten as a warrior, until you witness a feeding time when there's not enough of mother's milk to go around.

BALA BILIKASANA

Literally translated as *Child Cat Posture*,
felines prefer the more succinct *Kitten Pose*.
Very young kittens are known for their
tripping and stumbling, and this pose helps
them to develop the grace and balance
for which cats are renowned.

BALA BAKA DHYANASANA

The *Baby Crane Pose* improves a young kitten's sense of balance while stimulating development of the upper arms. In kittens these muscles are needed to bat balls of yarn and massage the mother while nursing.

BALA URDHVA UBHAYA HASTASANA

Like the adult version of the *Extended Two-Hand Posture*, this pose allows young yogis to extend their height and explore their new world from a different perspective.

Acknowledgments

My love of cats developed early in my childhood, and for that I must thank my mother and father for always having these wise and gentle creatures around our home as I grew up.

My warmest thanks go to the stars of this book: New-cat, Angus, Lino, Sadie, Ernie, Greystoke, Pearl, Rocky, Buddy, Jeremy, Thomas, Huffer, Cici, Louie, Oreo, Nathaniel, Candy, and their owners for sharing their time and helping this "pet project" of ours come to fruition.

Taking over one thousand pictures of cats requires time, patience, and a sense of humor. For that my deep gratitude to Dave and Pam Carroll of The Photique of Pismo Beach for taking such beautiful pictures and making the cats and their owners always feel welcome and at home in the studio.

Thanks to my agents Carolyn and Ashley Grayson for believing in the idea and finding a home for the book. Thanks also to Adrienne Jozwick and all the other folks at Clarkson Potter that helped this book along.

Special appreciation goes to my friend and collegue Tarn Shea. Without his image-editing artistry and personal training sessions this project would never have gotten off the ground. Assisting in the artistry department, warm thanks to Maggie Ragatz for helping with the composition of the images and backgrounds.

To my brother Chris, thanks for your initial enthusiasm for my silly idea which convinced me that I should pursue the project.

Cats need a place to practice yoga, and thanks to Michael Bengry and Golden Tree Yoga Studio in Santa Barbara we were able to get some wonderful environments for the cats to appear in.

Thanks finally to my mom for her unwavering excitement, enthusiasm, and support for the idea.